POETRY OF SOMEONE

POETRY OF LOST ERA

OM PRATAP SINGH

Made with ♥ on the Notion Press Platform
www.notionpress.com

To my family, who have always supported and encouraged my love of poetry. Thank you for believing in me and helping me to pursue my dreams.

And to the natural world, which has been my inspiration and my solace. Thank you for your beauty, your wisdom, and your endless capacity for renewal. May we always strive to protect and preserve the wonders of the earth.

I would also like to dedicate this book to all of the poets who have come before me, whose words have inspired and moved me. Your works have brought light and beauty into my life, and I am grateful for the rich tradition of poetry that you have left for us to continue.

And finally, I dedicate this book to anyone who has ever picked up a pen and allowed the words to flow from their heart. May these poems serve as a reminder of the power and beauty of the written word, and may they inspire others to continue the timeless art of poetry.

Contents

Foreword

In this stunning collection of poems, Om Pratap SIngh takes us on a journey through the natural world, exploring the beauty and complexity of the earth and its inhabitants. With delicate language and a keen eye for detail, he captures the full range of emotions and experiences that come with being a part of the natural world.

As you read these poems, you will be transported to a world of wonder and possibility, where the beauty of the earth is matched only by the depth of the human spirit. Whether you are a seasoned reader of poetry or new to the genre, I have no doubt that you will find something in these pages that resonates with you and touches your soul.

It is my great pleasure to introduce you to Om Pratap SIngh and his powerful and moving collection of poems. I hope that you will find as much joy and inspiration in these words as I have.

Preface

In this preface, I would like to share my thoughts on the process of creating this collection of poems and the inspiration behind them.

As a lifelong lover of poetry, I have always been drawn to the way that words can capture the beauty and complexity of the world around us. In this book, I sought to explore the connections between humanity and the natural world, examining the ways in which we are intertwined with the earth and all of its inhabitants.

The poems in this collection were inspired by my own experiences in the natural world, as well as by the works of other poets who have come before me. I have drawn upon a wide range of sources, from the delicate beauty of a flower to the raw power of a storm, in order to create a diverse and rich tapestry of poems.

It is my hope that these poems will inspire readers to look more closely at the world around them and to see the beauty and wonder that exists in even the smallest of things. I am grateful for the opportunity to share these poems with you and I hope that they will bring you as much joy and inspiration as they have brought me.

Acknowledgements

I would like to begin by expressing my deep gratitude to my family and friends, who have provided unwavering support and encouragement throughout the process of creating this book. Your belief in my work has been a constant source of motivation and I am truly grateful for your love and support.

I would also like to thank my editor, Kaushiki Singh, for their invaluable guidance and insights. Your expertise and attention to detail have helped to shape this collection into the book that it is today, and I am grateful for your dedication and hard work.

Finally, I would like to extend my thanks to all of the poets who have come before me, whose works have inspired and influenced me. Your words have touched my heart and awakened my soul, and I am grateful to be a part of the rich tradition of poetry. Thank you for your contributions to the world of literature.

Prologue

The poems in this collection are a reflection of my love for the natural world and the connections that we as humans have with the earth and its inhabitants.

Through these poems, I seek to explore the beauty and complexity of the natural world, delving into the deep and sometimes hidden connections between humanity and the environment. From the delicate petals of a flower to the raw power of a storm, these poems capture the full range of emotions and experiences that come with being a part of the natural world.

I invite you to join me on this journey, to explore the wonders of the earth and to discover the beauty and power of the written word. May these poems inspire you to look more closely at the world around you and to see the beauty and wonder that exists in even the smallest of things.

1. Just A Mango Grove

In the heart of the mango grove,
Where the trees stand tall and strong,
A sense of peace and wonder fills me,
As I wander among the leaves and fruit.
The sun shines down on the ripe mangoes,
Golden orbs of sweet delight,
Their fragrant aroma filling the air,
As the gentle breeze caresses their skin.
I am struck by the beauty of this place,
The way that the trees seem to reach for the sky,
Their branches full of succulent fruit,
A bounty of nature's abundance.
But as I look closer, I see the scars,
The marks of man's greed and destruction,
The trees hacked and mutilated,
Their lifeblood drained away.
And I am filled with sorrow and anger,
At the thought of such waste and neglect,
For this is not just a mango grove,
But a living, breathing part of our world.
But even in the midst of this devastation,
There is hope and renewal to be found,
As the mango trees continue to grow,

Their roots deep and strong in the earth.
And so I pledge to do my part,
To protect and nurture this land,
To care for the trees and the fruit they bear,
So that future generations may also enjoy their sweet delight.
For the mango grove is not just a source of food,
But a reminder of the interconnectedness of all things,
A reminder of our place in the natural world,
And our responsibility to care for it.

2. Horses In A Herd

In the fields of the wild and free,
Where the wind blows strong and steady,
The horses roam and graze and play,
A beautiful sight to behold.
With their manes flowing like rivers,
And their hooves pounding the earth,
They are a symbol of power and grace,
A reminder of the wildness in all of us.
But as I watch them run and play,
I am struck by their dignity and strength,
Their fierce independence and spirit,
A reminder of the beauty of the natural world.
For the horse is not just a creature of the earth,
But a partner and a friend,
A being with whom we share a deep and ancient bond,
A symbol of the bond between humanity and nature.
And so I honor the horse,
For all that it represents,
A reminder of the wildness in our hearts,
And the beauty and power of the natural world.

3. Nature's Revenge: The Cost of Pollution

In the cities of concrete and steel,

Where the smoke rises and the air is thick,

Nature has begun to strike back,

Against the poison we have wrought.

The rivers and the seas are choked,

With the waste of our excess,

And the skies are dark with pollution,

A toxic cloud that spreads and spreads.

The forests are cut down and burned,

Their beauty and their life destroyed,

And the creatures of the earth are dying,

Victims of our greed and pride.

But nature will not be silenced,

And she will have her vengeance,

As the storms rage and the earth quakes,

A reminder of the cost of our pollution.

For we are not separate from the earth,

But a part of it and bound to it,

And when we harm the earth, we harm ourselves,

In a cycle of destruction and despair.

So let us heed the warning of nature,

And work to heal the wounds we have inflicted,

Before it is too late, and the earth is lost,
To the ravages of pollution and greed.

4. The River's Song

In the fields of the wild and free,
Where the grasses dance in the breeze,
The river flows on and on,
A never-ending melody.
With its waters clear and cool,
It winds its way through the land,
A life-giving force of nature,
A source of beauty and of wonder.
As I sit beside its banks,
I am lulled by its gentle song,
A soothing sound that fills my soul,
And brings me peace and calm.
For the river is not just a body of water,
But a living, breathing being,
A part of the natural world,
And a reminder of its power and beauty.
So let us listen to the river,
And hear its song of life and renewal,
A reminder of our place in the world,
And our connection to the earth.

5. Climbing the Heights: A Mountain Adventure

In the depths of the wild and rugged mountains,

Where the air is thin and the winds are strong,

I set out on my great adventure,

To conquer the heights and prove my worth.

With my trusty pick and rope in hand,

I scale the steep and jagged walls,

Each step a test of my strength and courage,

As I push myself to the limit and beyond.

The higher I climb, the more I am humbled,

By the beauty and the power of the mountains,

As I gaze out at the world below,

I am filled with awe and reverence.

For the mountain is not just a challenge,

But a teacher and a guide,

A reminder of the strength and resilience,

That lies within us all.

And so I continue on my journey,

Pushed onward by my love for the climb,

Determined to reach the summit,

And claim my place among the heights.

6. The Power of Faith

In the face of fear and doubt,
When the world seems dark and cold,
I turn to the power of faith,
To guide me through the unknown.
For faith is like a beacon,
A light in the darkest night,
A source of strength and courage,
That helps me to keep the faith.
With faith in my heart,
I can overcome any challenge,
And find the strength to carry on,
No matter how difficult the path.
For faith is not just a feeling,
But a force that guides me forward,
A reminder of the love and grace,
That is always with me.
So let me hold on to my faith,
And let it guide me through the storm,
For with faith, I know that anything is possible,
And that I am never alone.

7. A Mother's Love

A mother's love is like a warm embrace,
A shelter from the storms of life,
A source of comfort and of strength,
In the face of fear and strife.
With a mother's love, we are never alone,
No matter how far we roam,
For her love is always with us,
A constant and unwavering force.
A mother's love is selfless and pure,
A sacrifice made without a cure,
For the happiness and well-being,
Of those she holds most dear.
And so, to all the mothers out there,
Who give so much and ask for nothing in return,
We thank you for your love and your devotion,
And for all that you do to make our lives worth living.

8. Nature's Price: Rise of Technology

In the age of technology,
We have made great strides and progress,
But at what cost to the natural world,
And the beauty and the peace it brings?
As we continue to advance,
And build our cities and our machines,
We pave over the earth,
And destroy the habitats of the wild.
The air is filled with pollution,
And the waters are choked with waste,
As we pollute and exploit the earth,
In our pursuit of power and control.
But nature will not be silenced,
And she will have her vengeance,
As the storms rage and the earth quakes,
A reminder of the cost of our technology.

9. The Tragedy of Food Waste

In a world of plenty and abundance,
Where food is readily available,
It is a tragedy to see so much wasted,
While others go hungry and in need.
The fields are filled with fruits and vegetables,
Their colors and their flavors ripe and bold,
But they are plowed under or left to rot,
As we turn our backs on the hungry and the poor.
The shelves of our supermarkets are overflowing,
With an endless array of choices and options,
But we take more than we need,
And throw away the rest without a thought.
And so, the cycle continues,
As we waste and consume without thought,
Ignoring the true cost of our actions,
And the suffering of those in need.

10. A Friend Worth Keeping

A friend is a treasure,

A source of comfort and of joy,

A loyal companion,

And a source of love and loyalty.

For a pet is a friend,

A being of pure and unconditional love,

Who greets us with wagging tail,

And never judges or holds a grudge.

With a pet, we are never alone,

For they are always by our side,

Ready to listen and to comfort,

With a gentle nudge or a soft purr.

And so, we must cherish our pets,

For they are a gift and a blessing,

A friend worth keeping,

For all the days of our lives.

And when our time on earth is done,

And we must say goodbye,

Our pets will be there with us,

To the very end, with love and grace.

For a pet's love is eternal,

A bond that can never be broken,

A reminder of the beauty and joy,
That they bring into our lives.

11. The Joys of Childhood

In the days of childhood,
When the world is new and bright,
We are filled with wonder and excitement,
As we explore and learn and grow.
In the warm embrace of our families,
We are safe and loved and cared for,
And we are free to dream and to imagine,
To be who we want to be.
The joys of childhood are many,
From the simple pleasures of a sunny day,
To the thrill of a new adventure,
And the discovery of something new.
And though the years may pass,
And we may grow and change,
The memories of our childhood,
Will always be with us, like a treasure.

12. The Final Journey

In the end, we all must face,
The great unknown of death,
A final journey that we must take,
To a place beyond our breath.
But death is not the end,
For life goes on in some form,
A continuation of the soul,
To a new and different norm.
So do not fear the final journey,
For it is a natural part of life,
A transition to something greater,
Beyond the pain and the strife.
And though we may not understand,
The mysteries of death and beyond,
We can find comfort in the knowledge,
That our loved ones are never gone.
For they live on in our hearts,
And in the memories we hold dear,
A reminder of the love and joy,
That they brought into our lives, here.